I IS FOR IRELAND

AN ALPHABETICAL TOUR

Copyright © 2011 by Viki Pidgeon
Publishing Rights: Pidgeon's Press
              140 Hunters Lane
              Simpsonville, KY 40067
              (502) 722-5588

13-digit International Standard Book Number: 978-0-615-49191-2
Library of Congress Control Number: 2011909664

Cover design and book layout: Patricia Prather
Illustrator: Heather Drury

Publication date: September 2011
Plant & Location: Printed by Everbest Printing (Guanghzhou, China), Co. Ltd
Job/Batch #: 97335

Printed in China

I is for IRELAND
AN ALPHABETICAL TOUR

BY VIKI PIDGEON • ILLUSTRATIONS BY HEATHER DRURY

A a

A is for abbey. During the 12th and 13th centuries abbeys were built throughout Europe and Ireland is a part of Europe. These ancient abbeys were home to religious groups of monks and nuns. There were various buildings within the walls of the abbey. A dormitory, kitchen, dining area, guest house, and of course, a church were some of the buildings on the abbey grounds. There were also gardens for growing fruits and vegetables. Kylemore Abbey is pictured. It is in the west of Ireland and is the oldest Benedictine abbey in Ireland.

B b

B is for the Book of Kells. The Book of Kells is a beautiful, 9th century Irish manuscript containing the Four Gospels in Latin. Most likely two people took part in the writing and illustrating of the manuscript. The colors used throughout the book are rich and vivid. Pages are filled with various unique illustrations of men, animals, and birds, as well as crosses, vines, dragons, fish, and serpents. The Blessed Virgin and the Divine Child are especially beautiful. The Book of Kells is on display at the Old Library at Trinity College in Dublin, Ireland. Every three months the volumes are changed or pages are turned.

C c

C is for castle. There is no shortage of medieval castles in Ireland. There are hundreds! Quite a few are in disrepair, but there are many that are still home to wealthy landowners. There are also quite a few castles that have been refurbished and are now lavish castle hotels. Dromoland Castle, Ashford Castle, Waterford Castle and Kinnitty Castle are a few of the magnificent castles offering overnight accommodations. There are others open for touring, such as Dublin Castle, Bunratty Castle, and Knappogue Castle. Each castle is unique in design, history, and size, and some of Ireland's castles are even thought to be haunted. Castles hold many dark secrets from the past.

D d

D is for Dublin. Dublin, Ireland's capital city, is located on the east coast of Ireland, is the largest city in Ireland and has the largest population. It is 118 square km (45.5 square miles) in area. And over one million people call Dublin home. The 125 km (75 mile) River Liffey flows through the center of Dublin. South of the Liffey are elegant Georgian townhouses with brightly colored doors. Usually ornate knockers are added, as well as elegant fanlights above the doors. Restaurants, hotels, pubs, museums, parks, and the prestigious Trinity College can be found in Dublin.

E e

E is for euro. On January 1, 2002 the euro became the official currency of the Republic of Ireland. There are 15 other countries in the Eurozone that use the euro as their currency. They are Austria, Belgium, Cyprus, Finland, France, Germany, Greece, Italy, Luxembourg, Malta, the Netherlands, Portugal, Slovakia, Slovenia, and Spain. The symbol for the euro is €. As mentioned, the Republic of Ireland uses the euro, but oddly enough, Northern Ireland does not, nor do the United Kingdom or Scotland, yet they are Ireland's close neighbors. These countries are on the British pound. The euro is divided into 100 cents, just like the American dollar. The denominations are 1, 2, 5, 10, 20, 50, 1 euro, and 2 euros, which are coins. The banknotes (paper money) are in denominations of 5 euros, 10 euros, 50 euros, and 100 euros.

F f

F is for fishermen and the fish they catch. There is a variety of reasons people fish Ireland's waters. The majority of fish are caught by commercial fishermen and are either exported or bought by restaurants and fish processors. Commercial fishermen fish with huge nets, whereas other people fish with a rod and line. Generally they are fishing for pleasure and sport, or to reap the rewards of a fresh fish dinner. Salmon and sea trout are abundant in Ireland's rivers and loughs. Atlantic salmon, larger salmon known as 'Springers,' weigh an average of 4.80 kilograms (9 pounds). Irish grilse, or summer salmon, are smaller, weighing from 1.36 to 2.71 kilograms, (3 to 6 pounds). In 1874 a man by the name of Michael Maher caught a 25.85 kilogram (57 pound salmon) on the River Suir, a record that most likely will never be broken. Nowadays a 20 pound salmon is classified as a specimen fish.

G g

G is for Gaelic. One of the two official languages of Ireland is Irish Gaelic. The other is English. When the primary educational system was introduced the children were only allowed to speak in English, so the Irish Gaelic language gradually faded away. In recent years, however, various organizations are trying their best to keep the Irish Gaelic language alive. Signposts display both the English and Gaelic spellings of Ireland's cities, towns, and villages. There are a few regions where Irish Gaelic is spoken every day. Donegal, a good sized town in the northwest of Ireland has the largest Irish-speaking district in the country. The Gaelic word for welcome is *failte*.

H h

H is for high crosses. It was during the 7th century that high crosses also known as Celtic high crosses were introduced into cemeteries throughout Ireland. Cemeteries dating back hundreds of years dot Ireland's lush countryside and high crosses mark many of the graves in the cemeteries. Generally they are made of sandstone and vary in size and style. Some may be twenty feet tall and rather simple, while others are massive and very ornate with a circle in the design. The tallest high cross is located in Monasterboice, Ireland and is 6.5 meters (21 feet) tall.

I i

I is for Ireland, an island in the sea. The official name of Ireland is Eire, and oftentimes people refer to it as the Emerald Isle because it is covered with green valleys, fields, and pastures. The official languages are Irish Gaelic and English. There are two separate countries that make up the island of Ireland, with 26 counties in the Republic of Ireland and 6 counties in Northern Ireland. The entire population is about 5.5 million. How big is Ireland? The answer is about 84,500 square km (or about 32,500 square miles),with about 5,630 km (3,500 miles) of coastline. If you are familiar with America, Ireland is about the size of Indiana. There are mountains, woodlands, streams, rivers, lakes, beaches, and of course, all the different bodies of water surrounding the island. Ireland seems to have it all!

J j

J is for James Joyce. Born in Dublin, Ireland in 1882, James was the oldest of 10 children. Although he was born in Dublin he spent the last 30 years of his life traveling and living in various other countries. He died in Zurich, Switzerland in 1941. James Joyce was an Irish novelist but also wrote a play and a number of short stories. His most famous work is *Ulysses*, a novel which takes place in Dublin, revolving around a single day in June (June 16, 1904) in the life of Leopold Bloom. Despite the fact that *Ulysses* was a controversial book, it is ranked first on the list of the 100 best English-language novels of the 20th century by the Modern Library. On June 16th Joyce fans the world over celebrate 'Bloomsday.' During the celebrations readings from *Ulysses* are featured, as well as James Joyce look-alike contests and various literary activities.

K k

K is for knitwear. Weaving factories can be found throughout Ireland. Wool is sheered from the sheep and spun into yarn. Long ago spinning wheels were used to spin the wool into yarn, but this process has now become modernized. The yarn is then knitted into hats, scarves and jumpers (sweaters) or woven into fabric, which is then used in making blankets, jackets, and other garments. Wives of fishermen would knit dense, weather-resistant sweaters for their husbands called ganseys, and the ganseys would have decorative patterns. One of the popular patterns knitted into a fishermen's sweater was the Basket Stitch, which represents the fisherman's basket.

L l

L is for lambing season. Believe it or not there are 8 million sheep in Ireland. Sheep can be seen grazing in the valleys and high up in the mountains. They can also be seen on the roads, keeping cars from passing. Each spring new lambs are born during what is referred to as 'lambing season.' Sometimes the sheep farmers need to help the ewe (mother sheep) if she is having a difficult time bringing her new lamb or lambs into the world. It is common for sheep to have twins. Sheep farming is a lot of hard work, which includes watching after the herd of sheep, making sure they are healthy and have enough to eat, and protecting them from predators. Sheep farmers have sheep dogs to help with herding the sheep and moving them from one place to another. Even though the dogs are called sheep dogs, they have no resemblance whatsoever to sheep. Many of the dogs are collies.

M m

M is for music sessions. There are lots of pubs and lots of musicians in Ireland. Oftentimes in the evenings the musicians get together and play music in the pubs. During and after a music session one might hear people say to one another 'good craic,' which is the Irish expression for good fun. Some of the instruments played in a "session" might include a fiddle, flute, tin whistle (penny whistle), a bodhran, and a small harp, which can be held on the musician's lap. While most sessions revolve around the playing of music, you may be treated to someone singing a ballad. It is customary to be quiet when someone stands up to sing. Everyone seems to be in a festive mood during a music session. And in Ireland children are allowed in pubs.

N n

N is for Northern Ireland. Northern Ireland is in the northeastern part of the island and is part of the United Kingdom. There are 6 counties in Northern Ireland: Counties Antrim, Armagh, Down, Fermanagh, Londonderry and Tyrone. County Fermanagh has more rainfall than any other county in the entire Island. The land is mountainous and has numerous lakes, attracting fishermen from all across the globe. The busy city of Belfast is the capital. And on a clear day Scotland can be seen in the distance.

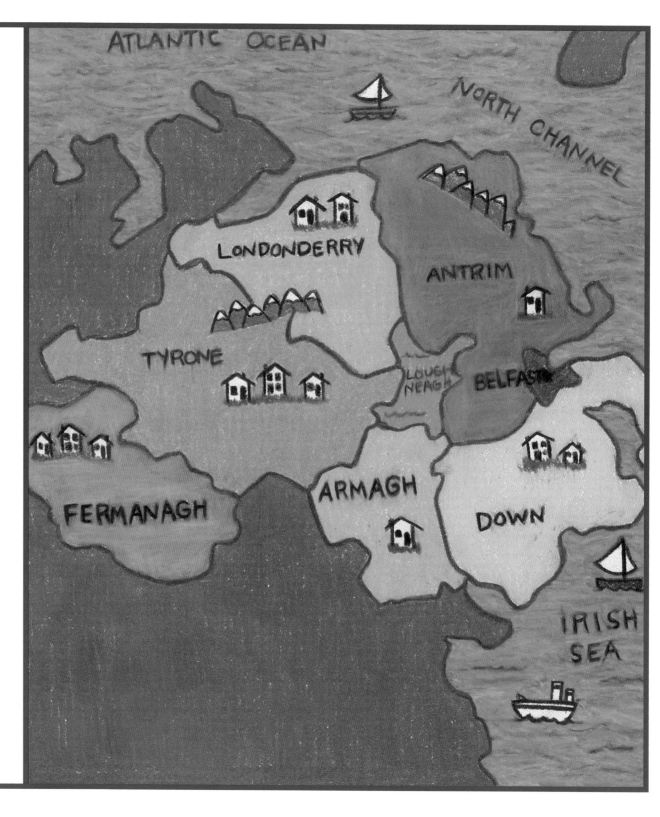

O o

O is for oysters and oyster festivals. As mentioned earlier, Ireland is an island. Naturally with being an island tons of fish,and shellfish are caught daily by all the fishermen. During low tide oyster farmers harvest oysters. There are more than 200 oyster farming operations in Ireland. More oysters are harvested during September, and October than during other months of the year, and that means it's oyster festival time! The Galway International Oyster Festival (which has been celebrated since 1954) features the Guinness World Oyster Opening Championship. Competitors from all around the world arrive in Galway for this event. The Clarenbridge Oyster Festival and the Hillsborough Oyster Festival are two other of the more popular oyster festivals. Oyster festivals offer oyster opening (shucking) and oyster eating contests, along with music and family fun for everyone.

P p

P is for potatoes. During the early 1500's Spanish conquerors took potatoes to Europe. Soon thereafter the potato was taken to England and eventually on to Ireland in about 1590. The rich, fertile land of Ireland proved to be excellent soil in which to grow potatoes. Loads and loads of potatoes were planted each spring and harvested in the fall. Potatoes were the main food in the diets of poor Irish families. Unfortunately in 1845 the potato blight hit Ireland and potato crops across the country were ruined. Food became harder to find. What resulted was starvation and disease followed by mass emigration. The 'potato famine' was a sad time in Ireland's history. Potatoes once again thrive in Ireland's cool, rainy weather, along with other fruits and vegetables.

Q q

Q is for Queenstown. Queenstown, Ireland was the last port of call for the ill-fated Titanic. On April 10th 1912 the Titanic left Southampton, England and docked to pick up passengers at Cherbourg, France. On April 12th the Titanic picked up about 120 passengers in Queenstown, Ireland. Most of the Irish passengers were traveling 3rd class (steerage) with dreams of a new life in America. Unfortunately, on April 14th at 11:40 PM the Titanic grazed a huge iceberg and within 3 hours sank. Of the 2,227 passengers only 705 were rescued. Few Irish passengers survived. Anna Kelly, a young 16 year old Irish girl did survive and later became a nun. The last survivor of the Titanic, Elizabeth Gladys "Millvina" Dean, of England, died at the age of 97 on May 31, 2009. "Millvina" was 9 weeks old when she set out on the Titanic's tragic voyage. Queenstown's Irish name is Cobh and is on Ireland's east coast.

R r

R is for round towers. Round towers were most likely built between the 9th and 12th centuries and can be found along Ireland's coast as well as inland. Generally round towers were built of stone and were located close to churches or monasteries. Even though the towers are centuries old, some are still in excellent shape. The towers are between 18-40 metres high (60-130 feet) and the tower door is about 3.048 metres (10 feet) off the ground. Which raises the question – how did people get inside? They would climb a ladder, then pull the ladder inside after them for security. One of the reasons for building round towers was to use them as bell towers. The Gaelic word for round towers is *cloictheach*, which means bell house.

S s

S is for Saint Patrick, Ireland's patron saint. Patrick was born in Wales. Somewhere between the age of 14 to 16, Patrick was captured by Irish raiders who took him to Ireland. For the following six years he lived in Ireland as a slave before escaping and returning to his family. After studying to be a priest, possibly at the monastery and school of divinity Cor Tewdws, Patrick returned to Ireland to spread the gospel message. He "baptized thousands of people," (his own words written in a letter). He also ordained priests to help spread the new Christian teachings. It is believed that Saint Patrick was born in 390 AD and died on March 17, 460 AD. Hence, Saint Patrick's Day is celebrated on March 17th each year. Around 441 AD Saint Patrick is said to have climbed Croagh Patrick, a holy mountain in the west of Ireland in County Mayo, and spent 40 days of Lent there. Every year on the last Sunday of July, about 30,000 people arrive at Croagh Patrick to make the annual pilgrimage to the top.

T t

T is for thatched roof cottage. Thatched cottage roofs were made of reeds because wood was so scarce. Not too very long ago thatched roof cottages could be found throughout Ireland. But little by little they are vanishing from the countryside. What were once quaint cottages are now roofless buildings with crumbling walls. There is a unique thatched roof cottage in County Tipperary known as the Swiss Cottage. It was built by Richard Butler, 1st Earl of Glengall, in the early 1800s. The Earl and his family used the cottage for picnics to which they brought their servants. The Butler family led a charmed life.

U u

U is for underground burial mound. Newgrange, located in beautiful County Meath, has become world famous as one of the oldest signs of primeval civilization and is the world's oldest solar observatory. Once a year at this mysterious burial chamber light shines through an opening of the "passage grave" for a few minutes on December 21, during winter solstice. Newgrange is older than the Egyptian Pyramids. The mound is 6 metres (20 feet) high and dates back to 3200 BC.

V v

V is for Vikings. Vikings from Scandinavia invaded Ireland in 1795. The need to create new settlements was the reason for the invasions. The first of the yearly attacks was on an Irish monastery (monasteries were often the targets of invasions) in Rathlen Island in the County Antrim area. The invasions, which were mainly along the coast, went on for 30 to 40 years. Around 1014 the majority of Vikings left Ireland. In 1038 King Sitric Silkenbeard, the Danish Viking King of Dublin, started building the Christ Church Cathedral. It was built on high ground overlooking Wood Quay, a Viking settlement which is still standing today.

W w

W is for weddings. Irish weddings are chock full of Irish traditions and customs. Let's start with the harvest love knot. Young men and women would weave or braid plaits of straw into decorative knots and give them to the one they love as a token of their love. The women would wear them in their hair or on their lapel. The bride's bouquet and the groom's boutonniere may even have a harvest love knot along with a small cluster of shamrocks tucked in with the flowers. Irish and Celtic music will be played at the wedding reception for the guests to dance to. And…the groom just might be wearing a kilt. (A kilt is a pleated tartan skirt). Often times the bride and groom exchange Claddagh rings as a symbol of their love. The Claddagh ring has three symbols: a heart representing love, hands representing friendship, and is topped with a crown for loyalty.

X x

X is for Xmas, or Christmas. Christmas in Ireland is a very special time of year. There's a lot of work to do on the days leading up to Christmas. The buying and wrapping of presents, the decorating of the house and Christmas tree all add to the festive mood of Christmas. Shopping for and preparing the food for Christmas dinner is a job in itself. The dinner will be the most lavish dinner of the year and will consist of all kinds of delicious foods. Foods such as turkey, ham, spiced beef, and the Christmas goose are some of the more popular meats served. Add in the stuffing, potatoes, cranberry sauce, Brussels sprouts, carrots, and Irish soda bread, and you have a meal fit for a king. Let's not overlook Christmas cake and Christmas pudding when dessert time rolls around. Typically presents are opened on Christmas morning, and the family will attend church together. Oftentimes there is a choir. Later in the day everyone will feast on Christmas dinner. *Nollaig Shona Duit* is the Gaelic way of saying Merry Christmas.

Y y

Y is for Yeats. William Butler Yeats was born in Dublin on June 13, 1865 and died on January 28, 1939 at the age of 73. Soon after William was born, his family moved to Sligo, a fairly large town in the west of Ireland. William began studying poetry during his youth. He never lost his thirst for knowledge. In 1923 William won the Nobel Prize for Literature. There are four Nobel Prize winners for Literature from Ireland, quite amazing considering the size of Ireland. The three other winners are George Bernard Shaw, Samuel Beckett, and Seamus Heaney.

Z z

Z is for Zodiac signs. There are 12 zodiac signs and a symbol for each one. All of the zodiac signs are important when it comes to farming, and Ireland has more than its share of farmers. For generations farmers all over the world have looked to the zodiac signs to guide them in determining when to plant various vegetables, grains, and flowers. Certain signs are better than others when it comes to planting. The farmers also look to the zodiac signs for plowing and cultivating their fields, harvesting the crops, cutting hay, weeding, pruning, weaning cattle, and breeding livestock. The Taurus zodiac sign is good for planting any garden vegetable that grows underground, a root crop, such as potatoes.

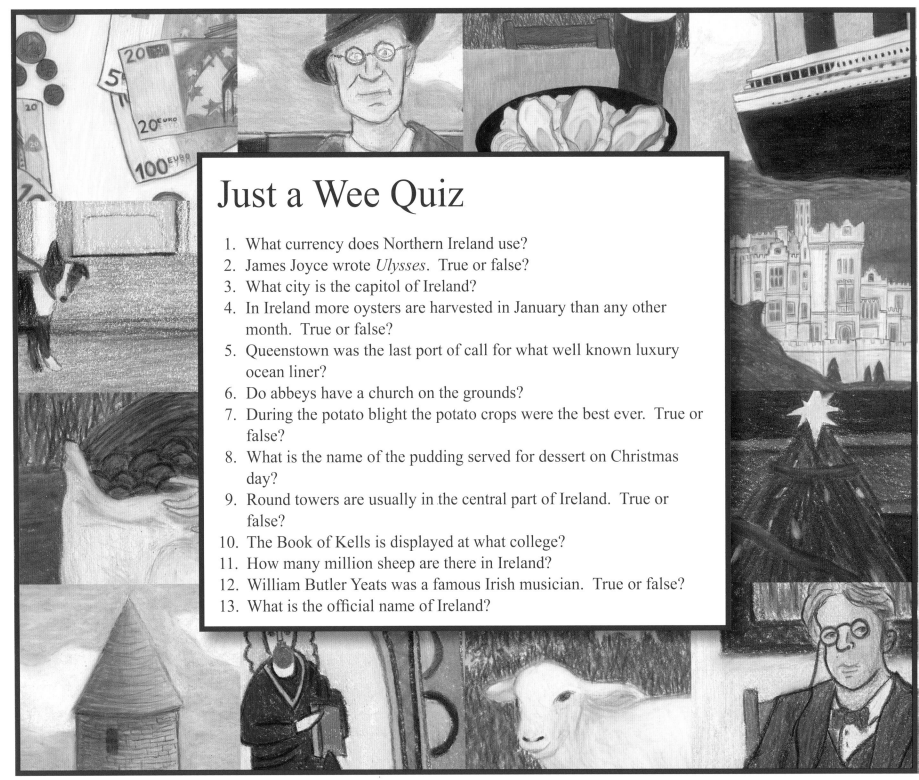

Just a Wee Quiz

1. What currency does Northern Ireland use?
2. James Joyce wrote *Ulysses*. True or false?
3. What city is the capitol of Ireland?
4. In Ireland more oysters are harvested in January than any other month. True or false?
5. Queenstown was the last port of call for what well known luxury ocean liner?
6. Do abbeys have a church on the grounds?
7. During the potato blight the potato crops were the best ever. True or false?
8. What is the name of the pudding served for dessert on Christmas day?
9. Round towers are usually in the central part of Ireland. True or false?
10. The Book of Kells is displayed at what college?
11. How many million sheep are there in Ireland?
12. William Butler Yeats was a famous Irish musician. True or false?
13. What is the official name of Ireland?

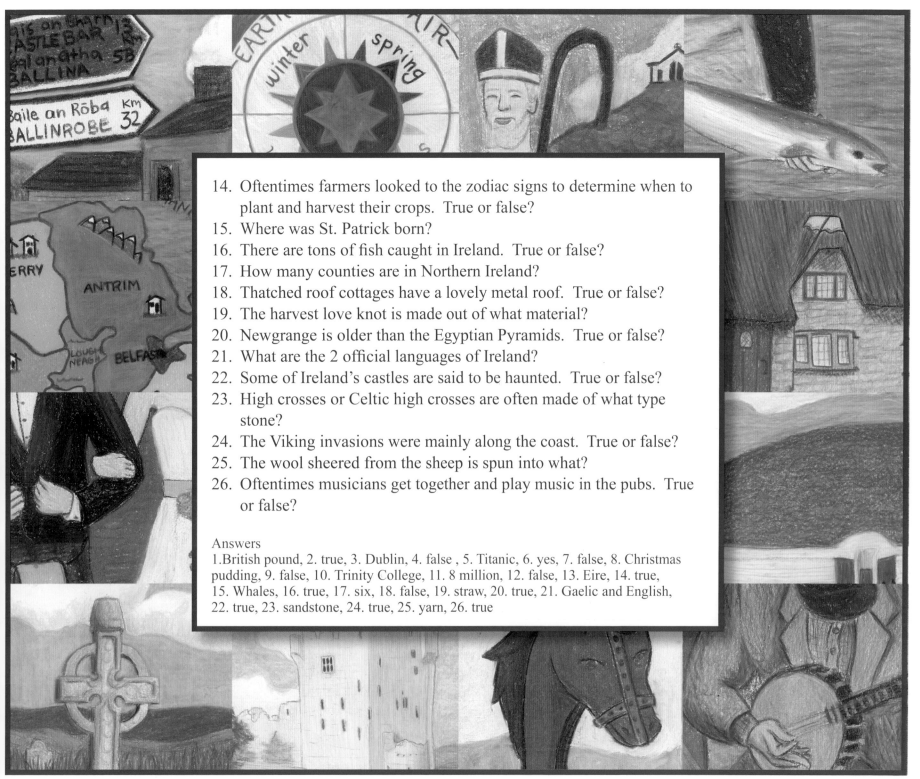

14. Oftentimes farmers looked to the zodiac signs to determine when to plant and harvest their crops. True or false?
15. Where was St. Patrick born?
16. There are tons of fish caught in Ireland. True or false?
17. How many counties are in Northern Ireland?
18. Thatched roof cottages have a lovely metal roof. True or false?
19. The harvest love knot is made out of what material?
20. Newgrange is older than the Egyptian Pyramids. True or false?
21. What are the 2 official languages of Ireland?
22. Some of Ireland's castles are said to be haunted. True or false?
23. High crosses or Celtic high crosses are often made of what type stone?
24. The Viking invasions were mainly along the coast. True or false?
25. The wool sheered from the sheep is spun into what?
26. Oftentimes musicians get together and play music in the pubs. True or false?

Answers
1.British pound, 2. true, 3. Dublin, 4. false , 5. Titanic, 6. yes, 7. false, 8. Christmas pudding, 9. false, 10. Trinity College, 11. 8 million, 12. false, 13. Eire, 14. true, 15. Whales, 16. true, 17. six, 18. false, 19. straw, 20. true, 21. Gaelic and English, 22. true, 23. sandstone, 24. true, 25. yarn, 26. true

Viki Pidgeon loves all things Irish! Learning more and more from each of her five Irish holidays she thought it important for others to learn about their Irish heritage. Having authored two Irish cookery books Pidgeon decided to create a childrens book with an Irish theme. What better way to learn about Ireland's history, heritage and culture than through the alphabet? Ireland is magical!

Viki was born and raised in Northern Ohio. After graduating from Solon High School she attended Morehead State University and Western Kentucky University. It was during her studies at WKU that she met her husband Barney. Both she and Barney hold dual citizenship in America and Ireland.

The author has two grown daughters. And lives on a farm in Simpsonville, Kentucky with her husband Barney, their dog Madison, thirty or so cows, and a menagerie of geese, ducks and various other critters.

Heather Drury recently graduated from Bellarmine University with a Bachelor's degree in Art and Sciences with an emphasis on painting. Her biggest inspirations come from her family and friends, and the beauty found in nature. Drury plans to continue her education and get her Master's degree in Fine Arts, to prepare her for teaching children of all ages how to create art from the world around them.
The illustrator lives in Louisville, Kentucky.